D1744698

The Secret of the
Cottingley Fairies

F.R. MAHER

FOR MUM & DAD

For tales of Tír na nÓg and fairies.

CONTENTS

Acknowledgments   i

1   In the Beginning   Pg 1

2   Believe it or Not   Pg 4

3   Once Upon a Time   Pg 8

4   A Wider World   Pg 15

5   Sir Arthur Conan Doyle   Pg 23

6   The Duping of Conan Doyle   Pg 41

7   Elsie & Frances   Pg 51

8   The Money   Pg 56

9   Confessions   Pg 62

10   The Reveal   Pg 77

ACKNOWLEDGMENTS

With thanks to Dan Baines, John Hyatt and Janet Bord, all friends of the Fae. Sincere thanks to Neil Rees for his cover design. Thanks also to the kind researchers and staff at the Brotherton Collection, Leeds.

1 IN THE BEGINNING

... But then poets and faeries have always been on terms of warmest camaraderie.

LORD DUNSANY

Despite their oftentimes fierce reputation in traditional stories, the fairies have always been very good to me.

A few years ago, I was looking for a 'new antagonist' for a proposed fantasy novel. After all, we have had a host of spangly vampires and a legion of zombies, so who or what might be the next enemy?

That is when I considered the fairies. Not the cute and helpful Disneyesque creatures or the magnificent elves of Tolkien, nor even the extraordinarily energetic *devas* of Findhorn, but the malign creatures of ancient legend.

Dark faeries have been the enemy of mankind since storytelling began. They haunted hilltop forts and other ancient sites demanding no human should cross their frontiers.

Woe betide anyone who did; they would become enchanted believing they had sojourned in Fairyland for just a few hours whilst above, in the real world, centuries passed. The 'lucky' ones emerged to find everyone they had ever loved were all long dead. Even Bridget, away for only seven years in the poem by John Allingham, did not escape the fairy curse:

They stole little Bridget for seven years long,

When she came back again, her friends were all gone.

They took her lightly back, between the dawn and morrow,

They thought that she was fast asleep,

But she was dead from sorrow.

In British and European legends, the fairies were much feared. They were beings that stole children and left wizened likenesses in their place, or who danced people to death and milked cows through a sieve – a particularly wicked practice when the average medieval peasant fought so hard for every resource.

Fairies, able to shape-shift and enchant, would be an incredibly effective enemy. Imagine if a modern mother began claiming her new baby wasn't hers? No one would believe her. But

2

what if she was right and her real child *had* been taken?

Thus my novel, *The Last Changeling* was conceived and written. Despite being self–published, it had sold over eight thousand copies to date – a respectable number for a previously unknown writer. As an offshoot and to promote my book, I created what has become an annual event, *The Legendary Llangollen Faery Festival.*

Held every year in mid-August in North Wales, UK it draws hundreds of traders and thousands of visitors. At time of writing it is now in its fifth year and had grown to be one of the largest fairy gatherings in the UK.

As I said, the fairies have always looked after me.

If what I am about to reveal dismays you, please remember, I'm *not* seeking to prove *or* disprove the existence of the Fae.

But, if you *do* believe, of all people, surely it is you who will

appreciate how much of what follows will appeal to the fairies trickster nature!

2 BELIEVE IT OR NOT

As Tolkien once said, *this is a tale that grew in the telling.*

It started when confirmed hoaxster, Dan Baines, creator of *The Derbyshire Mummified Fairy,* asked me to give a talk to mark the centenary of the affair of the Cottingley Fairies and their celebrated photographs.

I began researching the well known story of the two girls and their fairy photographs but within days I came across a stunning revelation.

On a recent trip to the literary town of Hay on Wye, (if you are a book lover and have never visited this pretty town stuffed full of bookshops, *go!*), I had pretty much bought my own body weight in old books on fairies and fairy lore. Within one of them I found some startling evidence.

Evidence that appears to have been overlooked for a century.

Initially I found the text confusing as it did not match any picture it purported to describe. I contacted the author and she revealed a further image had been cut from the text prior to publication. This would prove extremely important and difficult to track down, but more of that later.

Dan Bain's event, *Doomsday North*, was held in May 2017 in the dramatic setting of Sneaton Castle in Whitby, Yorkshire. It is there that I first revealed my findings when I addressed the *Doomsday* attendees – a closed gathering of top class magicians from all over the world. They were stunned.

One magician who uses copies of the photographs in his routine was dumbfounded. None of them were aware of the one hundred year old 'fresh' evidence. Not one of us, and I include myself, could quite understand why no-one had ever joined up the dots in the manner I have done before.

I had already contributed a couple of articles to *The Fortean Times* and a scant month after *Doomsday North*, I was commissioned to write a feature to mark the Cottingley Centenary. I do not believe the editor, Dr David Sutton realised how difficult it would be for us to secure permissions to publish this extra evidence. Two university faculties had to be consulted and neither appeared to know what the other was doing. At first both denied owning a particular image. Eventually it was located in a specialist collection.

I had to contact the guardians of one collection and submit my request to view their material two working days in advance; this was to allow sufficient time for the archivists to locate the pieces. After undertaking a journey of many hours to examine the evidence, I arrived exhausted to be told critical pieces could not be found. Heart sink; maybe the fairies had stolen them?

At least plenty of the other items I had requested to view had been found. Whilst the archivists hunted for the missing evidence, I sat in a featureless room like something from a Cold War movie, waiting. Each box of papers and photographs I had asked for had to be weighed in and weighed out again in case I suddenly decided to purloin the smallest scrap.

Whilst I waited for the lost papers to be located, I leafed through the dozens of letters that had passed between the principal players in the Cottingley incident.

A thrill of excitement passed through me as I held letters covered in Sir Arthur Conan Doyle's neat, rounded handwriting. *He had touched this.* Although his is not the easiest script to read, I have become accustomed to his style from looking at reproductions and I deciphered his notes with little difficulty.

Unfortunately, some of the letters have been damaged over the years. Many of Gardner's letters were kept in an old suitcase where the damp had got to them, but even so, I discovered clues that I do not believe have been put together before.

Eventually, I secured permission to reproduce the key pieces and that is why you are reading this now.

3 ONCE UPON A TIME

The year 2017 marked the centenary of one of the most celebrated events in fairyology.

Once again the story was dusted off and books and articles retold the tale about the little girls who photographed fairies in a Yorkshire dell. Though to some extent, the story never really went away. Over the years numerous books, newspaper articles, television documentaries and films have been made on the subject.

When the immensely popular series *Sherlock,* a modern re-imagining of Sherlock Holmes was first broadcast, his creator, Sir Arthur Conan Doyle came under fresh scrutiny. A slew of newspaper articles exposed his links to the Cottingley Fairy Photographs to a new generation of readers.

Most of them dismissed Doyle as a. bamboozled idiot whose interest in fairies, the afterlife and mediumship indicated a once fine mind now run to fat in late middle age. One article appeared under the unflattering headline: *Sherlock's Creator was Away with the Fairies...*

For those unaware of the events that unfolded at Cottingley, the story runs thus:

One hundred years ago, in 1917, two young cousins, Elsie Wright and Frances Griffiths were delighted to discover fairies flitting about Cottingley Beck, a woodland stream that ran behind their houses in the small Yorkshire town of Cottingley.

Frances was continually returning home with her clothes soaking wet after tumbling into the beck. Her mother would sometimes even beat her, so every time she fell in, Frances would cry, knowing that at the very least a severe scolding would be waiting for her at home.

Her cousin Elsie came up with the idea that if they could prove they had seen the fairies at the beck, and that it was merely Frances' curiosity that had led her to lean so far as to fall in, then perhaps she might be forgiven in future?

Elsie's father, Arthur Wright, was a keen amateur photographer and proud owner of, amongst others, a Midg camera. He had also created his own dark room in the cramped space beneath the stairs of his house. One early afternoon in July, the girls begged to borrow it. Though of the same era as Kodak's Box Brownie, which used film, the Midg employed glass plates to create negatives. Home for his lunch, Arthur loaded a single plate into the camera and the girls set off back down the steep sides of the beck to catch images of what they'd seen.

According to Elsie's mother, Polly, the girls were back within the hour, but they had to wait for Arthur to come home from work to see what they had captured on the glass plate.

At first, as the photographs developed, all Arthur saw were what he thought were scraps of paper, the 1920's equivalent of sandwich wrappers, and he scolded the girls for being so untidy, but then as the images became clearer, the scraps revealed themselves to be figures.

In a typed statement dated July 28th 1920, Arthur recalls:

... When I came in, in

the evening about 6 o'clock, Elsie said they "had taken a

photograph and would I develop?"

I did so and Elsie squeezed into my little dark room under the

stairs with me. When I saw the figures coming up I exclaimed "what have you been doing with this?" – but Elsie only called

out excitedly to Frances who was waiting outside the door, "the

fairies are on the plate! The fairies are on the plate!"

The picture clearly showed fairies dancing before Frances.
Arthur declared himself sceptical.

A couple of months later, in September 1917, the girls asked to
borrow the camera for a second time. Once again they were
give a single plate and this time little Frances took a
photograph of her older cousin Elsie apparently shaking hands
with what looked like a winged gnome.

Arthur developed the second plate, and bizarrely, very little fuss
was made over the pictures. Although Arthur claimed he and

Polly hunted high and low to uncover evidence that the girls had played some kind of a prank upon them. They searched the girls' attic bedroom for drawings or cut outs, they scoured the dustbins, they searched along the beck and up the embankment but found nothing incriminating. Eventually they gave up looking.

According to Joe Cooper in his 1990 book, *The Case of the Cottingley Fairies*, the glass negative plates and the sepia prints were stuffed away in a drawer and forgotten as a strange joke of some kind.

In 1918 Frances' soldier father, Sergeant Major Edwin Griffiths arrived back in England and shortly afterwards moved his wife Annie and daughter Frances to Scarborough in North Yorkshire.

The extraordinary photographs lay neglected for a couple of years. It wasn't until 1919 that they were revealed to the wider world – a world still reeling from the aftermath of the bloodiest conflict it had ever witnessed.

The First World War – at that time simply called The Great War – had shaken the foundations of society. For thousands, the triple pillars of Edwardian life, the sanctity of the home, knowing one's place and one's duty to God had become trivial irrelevances. Gender roles had been questioned as had the strictures of class, but even more so belief in a paternal deity. The horror of the trenches had left many asking how a merciful

God could overlook such abomination. People who had once called themselves Christian became agnostics or even atheists.

Into this widening religious void stepped the Theosophists, a group that in many ways mirrors a lot of modern spirituality. They had no dogma and only sought to focus on the central message of love from each of the organised religions.

The Theosophical Society had been set up in 1875 in New York, by Helena Blavatsky, Colonel Henry Olcott and William Quan Judge and was described as: *… an unsectarian body of seekers after the Truth who endeavour to promote Brotherhood and strive to serve humanity.*

Blavatsky was a medium and occultist. In the 1910's she declared she had *'lost her gift'* after finding she could no longer see a future for so many of the young men who came to her for readings. It was as if they were enveloped in utter darkness.

After the Great War with its huge losses, she said she must have been seeing the truth after all; for those young men there had been no bright future.

In just four years, the First World War had seen the natural order of things overturned on such a scale as it had never been witnessed before in the entire history of the world. Vast numbers of parents found that they had outlived their children when their sons were lost to the conflict. Little wonder then, that during those same years the number of spiritualist organisations in Great Britain doubled.

Along with many others, Elsie's mother, Polly Wright joined the Theosophical Society. Although she was neither a war widow nor seemed to have lost any close relatives in the war, Polly claimed, *'Theosophy has saved me from atheism.'*

4 A WIDER WORLD

In 1919, Polly attended a Theosophist meeting at Unity Hall in Rawson Square in Bradford, with her sister Annie, (Frances' mother), who was visiting from Scarborough. It so happened that on this occasion, the lecturer mentioned the subject of fairies. Polly approached the speaker afterwards and asked if the photographs her daughter and niece had taken might be accurate representations of an unknown realm?

At this time, the notion that cameras could *see what the human eye could not* was a widely held belief. Unscrupulous photographers had cashed in on the grief of many families shattered by the Great War, and *spirit photography* had become a lucrative venture for these charlatans. They would produce photographs of the sitter accompanied by another-worldly spirit or ghost of a relative who had been killed in action. It is possible that some thought they were offering a service to comfort the bereaved, but generally spirit photography appears to have been a heartless money making scheme.

Yet even the sceptics understood it was impossible to shake a grieving father's or mother's belief in such an image. My own grandmother, born a Victorian, died in 1961 in her eighties. She had lost two little daughters, Rose and Iris, in 1919 when they drowned in a mill stream near our Warwickshire village. Ever afterwards she firmly believed every sparkling reflection on the ceiling was her girls' dancing. My mother recalled how she would get very cross if anyone pointed out the source of the reflection, such as sunlight glinting off a mirror or the water in a clear vase. Even when the source was revealed, as far as she was concerned, the reflections were those of Rose and Iris and she would not have it any other way.

This mindset is at odds with our evidence-based way of examining facts; but ours is a relatively new way of looking at things. When the fairy photographs were first shown publicly, they emerged against a backdrop whereby spirit photography was deemed perfectly acceptable by a society willing to accept the supernatural.

The Theosophist meeting in Bradford, was the first time the

fairy photographs were shared outside the immediate family. The lady speaker's reactions are unrecorded but the images must have caused something of a stir as they were later displayed at the Theosophists annual meeting in Harrogate in late 1919. Then, sometime in early 1920 they came to the attention of Edward Gardner, when the lecturer Polly had first spoken to sent him two small prints and asked for his opinion. Gardner was the President of The Blavatsky Lodge in London and a senior member of the movement. A scholar of fairy lore and keen fairy hunter, all Gardner ever wanted to do was to observe such beings 'in the flesh.' So, from the outset, he was not unbiased.

As might be expected, Gardner was enchanted by the photographs.

In February 1920 he wrote to Polly for the loan of the negative plates. They were retrieved from the Bradford Theosophists and sent to him for inspection. When he received the two quarter plates, he found that one was reasonably clear but the second one was severely under exposed.

He wrote to the family and fired off some questions.

Held in the Brotherton Library in Leeds University, Gardner's original notes still exist. Neatly handwritten in pencil and dated July 14th 1920, they are on the back of a piece of paper advertising *Smedley's Hydropathic Establishment, Matlock,*

Derbyshire. His questions run down the left side of the paper and he has added the answers as he received them on the right side of the sheet:

Photos

Want to know

Dates of 2 photos	*July 1917*	*Sept 1917*
Times of day	*3.30*	*5.00*
Exposure		*Gnome i/50th*
Distance	*4 ft.*	*8ft.*
Camera	*The Midg*	
Plate and Description	*(writing unclear) Rapid*	
Age of girls	*17. 10 in 1917*	

Taken photos

before or since?	*Yes but fogged*
How long seen fairies?	*Many years*

Different kinds?

Colours of bodies	*Very pale*
& clothing?	*Colours, mauve, green, pink*

What accounts

published?   *Only one paper*

Prints circulated?   *Few*

When she first began receiving correspondence from Gardner, Polly Wright sought the assistance of a lady she had met at a neighbour's house, Mrs. Edie Wright, (no relation), to help with her response. It is possible she was overawed by the attention of such a senior member of the Theosophical movement. Edie had been also been a member of the Bradford Theosophical Society but had left for 'private reasons.'

What those private reasons for leaving may have been and what was her motive in assisting Polly, I cannot say, but she began to correspond, on Polly's behalf, with Gardner about the photographs. It was Edie who sent the photographs and plates to him for his inspection.

Gardner was careful to employ someone he could trust completely with regard to the photographs; he chose photographic expert, Harold Snelling. When he approached Snelling's former employer, he was told: *'What Snelling doesn't know about faked photographs isn't worth knowing.'*

Gardner gave Snelling the first sepia print and the glass plate from which it was taken for inspection. Snelling set the plate upon a light box and examined it with powerful lenses. Garner records Snelling's summation in his 1945 book, *A Book of Real*

Fairies: The Cottingley Photographs and their Sequel:

This plate is single exposure. These dancing figures are not made of paper nor of any fabric; they are not painted on a photographed background – but what gets me the most is that these figures have <u>moved</u> during exposure ...'

Gardner also sent the first photograph, known as *Frances and the Dancing Fairies,* to another expert on faked photographs, Fred Barlow. Barlow examined it and wrote to Gardner on 28 June 1920, reporting:

I am inclined to think, in the absence of more detailed particulars, that the photograph showing the four dancing fairies is not what it is claimed to be ...

Apparently Snelling's verdict carried more weight.

Gardner decided the plates needed 'improvement.' In a note made many years later, Gardner explains this enhancement as 'shading.' In his own words:

'... I told them to make new negatives, (from the positives of the originals), and do the very best with them, short of altering them mechanically. The result was that they turned out two first class negatives which of course are the same in every respect as the originals except that they are sharp cut and clear and far finer for printing purposes.'

As will be seen, the results were decidedly not *the same in every respect as the originals.* The 'them' was Harold Snelling.

'Them' could also be an attempt to throw any future investigators off the scent, (which in itself is curious; as if Gardner is wary of his motives being questioned). Its deliberate vagueness could mean a local photographic studio, or even a bigger organisation. Later on in the story, Kodak became involved. Gardner also mentions *Ilford enlargement for shading,* in another early handwritten note – Ilford being a manufacturer of photographic film.

Somewhat confusingly, just at that time, Edie Wright had travelled down from Bradford to Ilford in London and shortly thereafter met Gardner in person. However, it is unlikely Gardner's note refers to Ilford as a geographical place.

During their meeting, Edie Wright passed on the information that the girls had not deviated in any way from their story; that their mothers' completely believed them and that both girls had played with the fairies at the beck *since babyhood.*

Undeterred by the other expert, Fred Barlow's continuing scepticism, Gardner secured permission to take the photographs on a lecture tour. To this end, Snelling made up a number of copies of the two images which were sold to the public at the rate of one shilling and sixpence for a small print and two shillings and sixpence for a large print. That is the equivalent of £3.55 and just under £6 respectively at current prices. Two shillings and sixpence was the average *weekly* wage for a farm labourer at that time, so these photographs were not cheap by any means.

Gardner also asked Snelling to make him lantern slides of the photographs. These were shown by him at his lantern lecture at Mortimer Hall, London.

A certain Miss E.M Blomfield attended. She was so taken by the story of the girls and their photographs that she bought two photographs and sent them to her cousin, with the following observation:

They looked too good to be true …

Her cousin, the recipient of the note and photographs, was the creator of Sherlock Holmes, Sir Arthur Conan Doyle.

5 SIR ARTHUR CONAN DOYLE

By an extraordinary coincidence, Sir Arthur Conan Doyle had been commissioned to write a piece on fairies for the Christmas edition of *The Strand* magazine.

Doyle was initially reserved regarding the photographs, as witnessed in his comment to psychical researcher, Sir Oliver Lodge: (distinguished physicist and wireless pioneer, the first Principal of Birmingham University), *we must both be on our guard.* However, Doyle also remarked that they had been taken:

... by two children of the artisan class, and that such photographic trickery would be entirely beyond them ...

Doyle wrote to Gardner:

Windlesham,

Crowborough

Sussex

22nd June 1920

Dear Sir,

I am greatly interested in the 'fairy' photographs which
really should be epoch-making if we can entirely clear up the
circumstances. I am going to Australia presently to lecture on
psychic matters, and I should much like to get copies, not for
exhibition, but for private use. It so happens that I am writing
an article on Fairies at present, and have accumulated quite a
mass of evidence. It will appear, I think, as one of 'The
Uncharted Coast' series in the *Strand*. I would willingly pay a
reasonable sum, say £5, to reproduce the pictures and this
would be a good way of getting them formally copy-righted
both in England and America, which I certainly think the father
of the girls should do.

If I might have one or two notes as to who he is, where he
dwells, the age of the girls, whether they are in any way psychic
and so forth, it would greatly help me in my description.

We are all indebted to you as the channel by which this has

come in to the world.

Yours sincerely,

A. Conan Doyle

Although Garner replied with enthusiasm, he had encountered problems with Polly and Arthur. They seemed disinclined to allow Elsie to take any further photographs. Arthur Wright in particular appeared to be the major block to any progress as he was very sceptical regarding the fairy images. Meanwhile, Polly took the opposing view and was steadfast in her belief in the photographs.

Doyle wrote back to Gardner with the following points. He requested:

1. *Definite leave to publish the photos from Wright.*
2. *Double sets of the photos for England & USA.*
3. *Verbatim reports of experts pro & con and leave to publish with names.*
4. *Your own report, with that I am well equipped.*

In reply, Gardner pledged to assist Doyle in any way he could. He repeated the things Edie Wright had mentioned, including that the girls had played with the fairies since babyhood, and he also proffered the following observation regarding the girls:

... the two are far better than one as the proximity of the aura as you probably know strengthens the very delicate etheric vehicle of the fairy and make it more actinic ...

In other words, Gardner believed that the presence of both girls was necessary for the fairies – who he believed to exist outside the visible spectrum – to be able to manifest in the visual realm.

Via Gardner, Doyle wrote to the Wrights. He sent a letter to Elsie dated the 30th of June 1920, promising to send her one of his adventure books. On the same day he also wrote to her father, Arthur, requesting permission to use the photographs alongside an article on the evidence for fairies in the *Strand*. Doyle offered £5 for *temporary* leave to publish the photographs, or a year's subscription to the magazine, with a further £5 from the American edition. He suggested no names should be used and apologised for not being able to visit them personally as his trip to Australia was imminent.

Arthur Wright took well over a week to answer. On the 12th of July 1920, he finally responded thanking Doyle for his daughter's book and explaining that Gardner had also written, proposing a visit at the end of July.

In the meantime, on the 5th. of July 1920, Sir Oliver Lodge had sent the photographs to Kenneth Styles, a psychic and a fairy authority.

Not only did Styles pronounce them a fraud, he also claimed he could recognise which studio they came from. He did not mention Snelling by name, but came close to claiming that they had been deliberately enhanced in a studio to make them look more like real fairies. He wrote to Doyle on 18 July 1920, saying:

.. Re photographs; the more I think of it the less I like it. My own controls say it was taken by a fair man with his hair brushed back. He has a studio with a lot of cameras some of which are turned by a handle. He did it to please the little girl in the picture who writes fairy stories which he illustrates in this fashion.

'Controls' here refers to Styles' spirit guides who appear to believe a man took the pictures. He also pointed out the modish *Parisienne* hairstyles of the fairies in the photographs.

However, Gardner's faith was unshakeable. In no small way it was his confidence in the photographs that prevented Conan Doyle from dismissing the matter entirely at the outset. Critically, Doyle never saw the original photographs taken from the original plates, just the prints from the 'improved' plates.

It was agreed that if the negatives gained a second favourable review from another expert – preferably Kodak – then the pictures would indeed become the centrepiece of Doyles's article for the *Strand.*

Gardner sent the negatives to Doyle and he presented them to Kodak. He personally saw Mr. West, Kodak's manager and photographic expert who examined the negatives at length. His summation was not as enthusiastic as Snelling's and he gave this statement:

Kodak were not willing to give any certificate concerning them because photography lends itself to a multitude of processes and some clever operator might have made them artificially.

At no point were Kodak given the original plates to examine. But someone noted:

... after all, as fairies couldn't be true, the photographs must have been faked somehow.

Yet, despite the original plan to get a positive second opinion, Kodak's verdict did little to deter Gardner's enthusiasm. His knowledge of fairy lore and the hundreds of sightings recorded over the centuries convinced him that fairies were real and this was the very proof he had devoted his entire life to finding.

Doyle was still a little wary. In one to his letters to Arthur Wright he suggested that if only Elsie could take another photograph it would:

... Silence the doubters ...

Yet Gardner chose to embrace only the positive comments

about the images.

He first visited Cottingley on the 26th. of July 1920, for a couple of days. He stayed overnight at the Midland Hotel, Bradford and the *Strand* magazine paid for his expenses plus £25 for the interview.

Gardner spoke to the Wright family at length. As Frances was by now living in Scarborough, he walked down to the beck with Elsie where he had his photograph taken by the waterfall to verify the site.

Arthur Wright told Gardner that Doyle could indeed use the photos in the Strand magazine, but firmly declined payment, saying that if the photographs were genuine they should not be *soiled by being paid for.*

Gardner returned to London certain that all involved were honest and respectable people. He wrote to Doyle that he was convinced of the sincerity of the Wright family and the veracity of their photographs. He sent Doyle the following statement:

THE FAIRY PHOTOGRAPHS

As stated verbally to Mr Gardner during his visit here on

July 28th. I confirm the following –

In July 1917, my daughter Elsie and her cousin Francis, who was staying with us at the time, begged me one day to let them

have my Midg camera. It was about 1 o'clock that I put just

one plate in the box and gave it to Elsie. When I came in, in

the evening about 6 o'clock, Elsie said they "had taken a

photograph and would I develop?"

I did so and Elsie squeezed into my little dark room under the

stairs with me. When I saw the figures coming up I exclaimed

"what have you been doing with this?" – but Elsie only called

out excitedly to Frances who was waiting outside the door, "the

fairies are on the plate! The fairies are on the plate!"

The plate I took out was certainly the one I put in that day and

my wife says the children were not gone an hour before they

brought the camera in saying they had taken a photograph.

Beneath this typewritten statement, Gardner scribbled the
following note:

I can't explain the photo for – (unclear name), doesn't
understand it, but this is a true statement of what happened.

Doyle was delighted with Gardner's findings. As he put it in a note to him:

… Your report is <u>admirable</u>. I could not wish for a better colleague …

Yet both men wanted further photographs. Gardner thought perhaps if he gave Elsie a camera of her very own, she could take pictures whenever she pleased without having to borrow her father's precious Midg? Gardner thought it could well re-invigorate the investigation. He sent her a camera, with secretly marked plates. Polly replied on the 15th.:

The camera and plates have arrived alright … Elsie is a very lucky girl! … it is a very handsome present … I do hope Elsie will be able to take some photos of the kind you want.

A few days later, Polly wrote this to Gardner:

… The camera you so kindly sent is fine, far better than those we have. I hope it isn't long before we can send you some photos of the kind you want…

In a matter of days, Gardner received the news he had hoped for. In a letter dated the 22nd of August, Polly wrote about the events of the preceding Thursday. It seems the day started dull with mist so no pictures could be taken until after lunch when the sun came out. Polly was away for most of the day, so she had left the girls to it.

When she returned, the girls had only managed to take two fairy photographs for which Polly declared herself 'disappointed.' Two days later, the girls visited the beck and the old reservoir – where they had seldom visited before. They took a few pictures, but only one had something on it.

Polly described this picture as *a queer one.* In her postscript she mentions that the girls:

... did not take one flying after all.

Again, Elsie's father, Arthur, developed prints from the three plates showing fairies, and returned them to Gardner who upon receipt, immediate took the three secretly marked plates to his expert, Harold Snelling.

Snelling decided they were as genuine as the first two and even declared that the final picture, the one Polly had described as *queer,* which is now known as *The Fairy Sunbath,* as being:

... utterly beyond any possibility of faking.

This time, Gardner ignored Kodak and went to Ilford's experts who agreed with Snelling – who had again enhanced and retouched the plates. Excited, Gardner sent a telegram to Doyle who was by then in Melbourne having left some weeks earlier on his lecture tour of Australia.

Whilst he waited to hear back from Doyle, Gardner kept up his

32

correspondence with Polly.   He must have been hoping for more photographs for his investment in a fine, new camera for Elsie, but Polly apologises for the lack of results due to various reasons: holidays, another niece staying, getting back too late from a day out, Elsie being busy or Elsie being ill.

About September 15th. 1920, (according to Gardner's handwritten annotation), Polly writes:

… I am writing on behalf of Elsie. She is on the sick list, she is not very strong. Your letter and parcel cheered her up ever so much. She was delighted with the chocolates, she says I must thank you ever so many times …

There were no more photographs, but there is this letter amongst Gardner's notes:

TWO PHOTOGRAPHS OF A GROUP OF FAIRIES AND A GNOME

TAKEN IN AUGUST AND SEPTEMBER IN YORKSHIRE AND THREE PHOTOGRAPHS OF FAIRIES (1leaping, 1 with flower in hand, and 1 showing bower) TAKEN IN AUGUST 1920 AND SEVERAL PLATES EXPOSED AT THE SAME TIME BUT UNSUCCESSFUL, BY MISS ELSIE WRIGHT AND HER COUSIN

We have not given anyone authority prior to this date

To use or publish these photographs. We now authorise

Edward Lewis Gardner of No. 5 Craven Road, Harlesden

London as our Sole Agent, to use and negotiate the

above described photographs in any way he may decide

as best towards making them public. Remuneration for

this authority we agree to leave in his hands –

Dated the 24th day of September 1920.

Following Gardner's telegram, Doyle eventually replied from Australia via a letter dated October the 21st. in which he enthuses:

My heart was gladdened when out here in Australia I had your note and the three wonderful prints which are confirmatory of our published results …

When our fairies are admitted, other psychic phenomena will find a more ready acceptance … we have had continued messages at séances for some time that a visible message was coming through …

… But anything which extends man's mental horizon, and proves to him that matter as we have known it is not really the limit of the universe, must have a good effect in breaking down

materialism and leading human thoughts to a broader and more spiritual level. It almost seems to me that those wise entities who are conducting this campaign form the other side, and using some of us as humble instruments, have recoiled before that sullen stupidity, against which Goethe said that the Gods themselves fight in vain, and have opened up an entirely new line of advance which will turn the so-called 'religious' and essentially irreligious position which has helped to bar out way. They can't destroy fairies by antediluvian texts, and when once fairies are admitted, other psychic phenomena will find a more ready acceptance.

Goodbye, my dear Gardner, I am proud to have been associated with you in this epoch-making event …

Even Fred Barlow, the leading authority on psychic photographs who had been so dismissive of the first two pictures changed his mind when he saw the new photographs. On the 12th of December he wrote the following to Gardner:

I am returning herewith the three fairy photographs you kindly loaned to me, and have no hesitation in announcing them as the most wonderful and interesting results I have ever seen.

Conan Doyle's article with the two original pictures appeared in the *Strand* magazine in December 1920. It received mixed reviews; but by no means to the universal scorn that's sometimes reported. As the 'epoch-making' news spread to other publications, the press saw how well the photographs sold newspapers and were careful not to kill the story.

Three months later Doyle wrote a second article in *The Strand* which was reproduced in his book, *The Coming of the Fairies.* But by the time it was published in 1922 with the third, fourth – and even more interesting – fifth image of the Cottingley fairies, *The Fairies Sunbath*, Doyle was an object of derision in some quarters. Yet he continued to revise his book for future editions; all the time amassing further arguments to strengthen his claims, including this:

It may be added that in the course of exhibiting these photographs, (in the interests of the theosophical bodies with which Mr. Gardner is associated), it has sometimes occurred that the plates have been curiously magnified upon the screen. In one instance at Wakefield the powerful lens used threw up an exceptionally large picture on a huge sheet …

The following was crossed out:

… increase was about fifty fold.

Doyle continues:

The operator a very intelligent man was getting converted to the truth of the photographs, for, as he pointed out, such an enlargement would show the least trace of …

The following is crossed out:

... a scissors cut.

And Doyle resumes with:

Irregularity of any artificial detail and would make it absurd to suppose that a dummy figure could remain undetected. The lines were always beautifully fine and unbroken.

I doubt if Doyle was present in Wakefield at one of Gardner's lantern slide lectures, therefore it seems likely that Gardner himself was the source of this extra 'evidence.' It is interesting that Doyle has finessed the account, cutting out the improbable 'fifty fold' reference and replacing the prosaic 'scissors cut' with the more impressive sounding, 'irregularity of any artificial detail.' Even Doyle was putting the most positive spin imaginable onto the story.

In early August 1921 Gardner went again to Cottingley as Doyle wanted even more proof. Doyle had suggested clairvoyant Geoffrey Hodson should visit too. An ex British Army Officer, Hodson, then aged 31 was akin to a proto hippy. He had explored the realms of yoga, healing, spiritualism and clairvoyance and was regarded as an expert in psychic phenomena. Sensitive and imaginative, Doyle considered him the perfect subject to detect any fairy phenomena.

Frances returned from Scarborough and Hodson and his wife

went ever day of their visit with the girls to the beck to look for the fairies. Gardner was not allowed to accompany them as he did not have the 'requisite gifts.'

What Gardner made of his exclusion is not reported, but it is unlikely the situation sat well with him. Were it not for his initial investigation, Doyle would never have heard about the Cottingley fairy photographs in the first place.

On the 3rd of August, Gardner walked three miles into the woods by himself looking for fairies. The next day he spied on the party, possibly hoping to share a fairy sighting with them.

His original notes record the following:

Tuesday Aug 2nd.

Arrived 1 pm. Showery. Rained heavily in afternoon. Frances at Cottingley. Elsie home in evening.

Wednesday Aug 3rd.

Cottingley 11.00. For most part fine. Glen after 2.00. Scout camp! Walked through glen. Elsie remarked on a different 'feeling' – left girls alone at willow for hour – nothing 'happened.' Walked on into woods, about 3 mile. 'No good' – home about 5.

Thursday Aug 4th.

Cool, windy, fine, dull. Cottingley 2.30. Girls had gone up Beck.

*Camp gone. Followed and 'spied' – they met 'nothing doing' –
left them to continue – girls came in about 5pm – no result.
Wet evening.*

Friday Aug 5th

Rained all day continuously. Returned in evening.

Saturday Aug 6th.

*Very windy – fine except 2 showers. Cottingley 1pm – girls by
beck at 10 am. Waited and they came home 1.30 – 'saw
nothing' – left to meet Hodson – arranged not to call till
Monday.*

Sunday Aug 7th.

Dull and rainy, (nothing).

Monday Aug 8th.

*Sunny intervals. Showery, high winds – Mr Mrs Hodson by
beck from 11.30 to 4.30. Power felt. Nothing seen.*

Tuesday Aug 9th.

*Mr & Mrs Hodson & girls. Fairly fine but overcast and windy –
nothing more.*

Whilst Gardner returned home to London, Hodson stayed on for
a few days reporting many sightings. He saw fairies dancing in
a field and wood elves beneath some beech trees.

In his 1925 book, *Fairies at Play*, Hodson recounts that he spent some time with both families and became convinced not only of the sincerity of the persons involved but also that the fairy photographs were genuine and that the girls both possessed very real skills of clairvoyance.

But for all of this, Hodson had not managed to facilitate the taking of a single photograph of fairies as evidence to back up his claims.

Although his detailed reports of the Cottingley sightings are cited in Doyle's *The Coming of the Fairies* and also appear in Gardner's later publication *A Book of Real Fairies*, Gardner was bitterly disappointed by the lack of further photographs.

6 THE DUPING OF CONAN DOYLE

Our ideas must be as broad as Nature if they are to interpret Nature.

Arthur Conan Doyle

It seems strange that Sir Arthur Conan Doyle, a man whose sharp mind had conceived that most celebrated detective, should have been fooled by two little girls. If anything, the character of Sherlock Holmes is founded upon his pride in his abilities of observation and deduction. Surely his creator would have some talent in that direction too?

Indeed he had.

Called upon to become a real-life consulting detective in the matter of *The Great Wyrley Outrages*, Sir Arthur Conan Doyle rose magnificently to the occasion, channelling pure Sherlock in a case that changed legal history.

In the early 1900's in the Staffordshire village of Great Wyrley, a series of poison pen letters began to circulate, much to the distress of their recipients. At around the same time a number of horses were attacked and mutilated in their fields.

The police didn't look far for a suspect, local solicitor George Edalji was known to wander the district at night. He was half-Indian, non-Christian and that was deemed enough evidence to convict him. George was sentenced to six years hard labour and let out after three years. He immediately sought Conan's Doyle's assistance in clearing his name.

Doyle had trained as an ophthalmologist. He employed his expertise to reveal how George's extreme short-sightedness would not have allowed him to easily cross a few miles of open countryside, nor find his way through hedges, let alone locate an un-tethered pony in a large field on a moonless night – and all within the only thirty five unaccounted-for minutes available to him to execute the dreadful deed.

The police, annoyed at Doyle's interference sought to discredit him with counterfeit letters, but Doyle saw through their fakery and persevered.

Edalji was eventually pardoned and it was partially due to this case that the Court of Appeal was established in 1907.

In 1909, Oscar Slater was found guilty of murdering elderly spinster, Marion Gilchrist. The prosecution made much of the fact that he had 'fled justice' in that Slater had left for America five days after the murder. They ignored the fact that he had made it known for some time before his trip that he intended going. He could have remained in America as, at that time, it was highly unlikely that he would have been extradited, yet Oscar willingly returned to clear his name.

In the police line up, he was sharply contrasted by nine off-duty policemen in his identity parade. Another line of enquiry concerning Slater's attempts to sell a pawn ticket for a brooch – a brooch had been stolen from Miss. Gilchrist – was also found to be a false lead. Yet Slater, considered a ne'er-do-well, found himself in the dock accused of murder and was convicted on a majority of nine to six. He was sentenced to death by hanging.

Slater's legal team organised a petition which 20,000 people signed. The Secretary for Scotland, Lord Pentland, issued a conditional pardon, commuting Slater's death sentence to life imprisonment.

In 1912, Doyle published *The Case of Oscar Slater* with a plea for his full pardon. However, it wasn't until 1928, after Slater had served nineteen years in prison, that his conviction was eventually quashed. He received £6,000 compensation.

It seems that the ophthalmic expertise that had so aided Doyle in the matter of George Edalji, was just one of the many elements that led him astray in the case of the Cottingley Fairy photographs.

He was of the opinion that children could see more than adults. This belief was not some half-dreamed, psychic ability borne of innocence and conjured up by the poets, but actual, *physical* sight. It seemed more than possible to him that children's eyesight was sharper than that of adults – an acuity that could, in certain subjects, extend beyond the visible spectrum.

This belief was prevalent amongst many as it was congruent with new scientific discoveries. A scant sixteen years before the Cottingley photographs had been taken, Wilhelm Roentgen had received a Nobel Prize for his work on *Roentgen Rays*, now better known as X-rays.

It must have been exciting to suddenly be able to see through flesh and peer inside solid bodies, and as this was still a relatively new discovery it suggested that there could be many more ways of seeing just waiting to be discovered.

In believing children can see more, Doyle wasn't a million miles from the truth. Children can certainly *hear* more than adults.

In 2005, in Barry, South Wales, Howard Stapleton's seventeen year old daughter arrived home in tears after being harassed by a gang of younger children loitering around the local Spar shop. Howard decided to do something about it. Unlike most dads, Howard's solution to the problem was distinctly refreshing. He did not march down to the shop and confront them; he did something that would stop them and any future would-be bullies once and for all.

Recalling how the noise from a local factory used to upset him as a child but left the adults around him unaffected, Howard set about replicating the effect. Ironically, he used his own children as guinea pigs to fine tune the irritating sound, but mercifully for them, before too long, *The Mosquito* was born.

This device emits high frequency sounds that children can hear, but adults can't. The Spar shop became the testing ground and sure enough, unable to bear the noise, the young loiterers dispersed.

This may demonstrate that Doyle's hypothesis about children's eyesight being keener was not unreasonable, but it was fatally untested.

He further compounded his error by falling back on Snelling's flawed expert analysis where he reported movement in the creatures' wings. But, undoubtedly, it was Snelling's retouching of the negatives that was the biggest pitfall when it came to the 'solid' evidence of the photographs.

Doyle's strong desire to promote spiritualism – a desire that ultimately cost him his friendship with Harry Houdini – augmented his willingness to accept the photographs as real. He considered this new evidence of the presence of fairies as merely a forerunner, a test upon mankind's ability to grasp supernatural matters. It was as if some universal and wise beings behind the scenes were drip feeding us the dainty fairies as heralds for further revelations.

Of the fairies he said:

The recognition of their existence will jolt the material 20th-century mind out of its heavy ruts in the mud, and will make it admit that there is a glamour and mystery to life .

Yet there was something more compelling than spreading the ideals of spiritualism that urged Conan Doyle to believe. But it wasn't, as some think, the loss of his son, Kingsley, in the Great War.

Rather like my own case, fairies were a family business for the Doyles. Richard *'Dicky'* Doyle, Arthur's uncle, was a famous illustrator of many fairy books, such as the series by Andrew Lang named after the colours of their covers: *The Yellow Fairy Book, The Violet fairy Book, The Green Fairy Book* and many more. Dicky also created the banner artwork for *Punch* magazine. It may have seemed strange to the casual observer that the heading for a satirical magazine should feature so

46

many fairy and goblin-like creatures playing around the lettering, but it served the magazine well, becoming its longest lasting banner and surviving up until 1958.

Doyle's father, Charles Altamont Doyle also had artistic leanings, but he was not quite as talented as his brother. Charles trained in architecture and designed a fountain at Holyrood Palace, but still drew fairies in his spare time.

Beset by self-doubt and depression, Charles drifted into alcoholism. When Arthur was still in his twenties, Charles was sent to a nursing home. Once there he succumbed to an even deeper depression and began suffering from epilepsy.

After a violent escape attempt, Charles was committed to *Sunnyside*, the bleakly named lunatic asylum at Montrose where he continued to draw all manner of *little people*. After all, Charles parents had been Irish and that is how he saw the fairies, diminutive figures without wings.

In Sir Arthur Conan Doyle, we have a man almost *genetically predisposed* to see fairies, having been brought up in a highly artistic household, with both his uncle and his father deeply interested in fairies and fairy lore.

Not sharing the family's facility for art, he turned to science to prove the existence of fairies.

Arthur clearly adored his father; an 1888 edition of the first

Sherlock Holmes adventure, *A Study in Scarlet* featured
illustrations by Charles Altamont Doyle. In the final Sherlock
Holmes story, *His Last Bow*, Doyle has Holmes use *Altamont*, as
an alias and in 1924, Doyle arranged an exhibition of his
father's paintings. These are hardly the actions of a man
embarrassed by his father's activities, or even his incarceration.

To have had a parent locked up in a lunatic asylum would have
left most late Victorian/early Edwardians filled with shame, and
reluctant to advertise their parent, let alone address any aspect
of that parent's mania.

That Conan Doyle should be actively celebrating his father by
promoting belief in fairies ran contrary to all the prevalent
societal restraints and niceties. It's a measure of how deeply
Arthur loved his dad that he did so.

Perhaps he believed dipsomania was just another way of
piercing the veil between the worlds? There could even be
redemption – if Doyle could only prove fairies existed, it would
mean his father might not be as crazy as everyone made out.

In 1926 *Punch* published a cartoon of Sir Arthur smiling
beneficently, his head wreathed in clouds of pipe smoke,
shackled to a pensive Holmes. Beneath it ran a poem lamenting
Doyle's fanciful ideas, (compared to Holmes cool logic), but
ending with real warmth and affection:

We sympathise with Holmes and yet, in Punch's heart your name is set.

Of every DOYLE he is a lover, for DICKY'S sake who did his cover.

In many respects, Doyle's 'scientific' rationalisations overlaid with loyalty to a father lost in alcoholism, and tempered by his desire for there to be a 'glamour and mystery' to life, primed him to be the perfect dupe. Even so, he might have drawn back from disaster had he not relied so heavily upon Snelling's summation that the photographs were single exposures with evidence of movement. Then there are the retouched prints being the focus of his investigation, not the original photographs.

When Gardner asked Snelling to 'sharpen' the negatives, he unwittingly laid the trap for Doyle to tumble into. Snelling was an expert on photographic retouching and he enhanced the original negatives to make finer prints. In doing so he removed shadows and lines which were later rediscovered in the original photographs and clearly show the figures as flat, two-dimensional cut-outs. Snelling made the fairies appear more rounded and real than they did in the original prints. He made them lighter with greater definition and although they fail to fool modern eyes, they would have seemed very convincing in 1920.

Regarding Snelling's verdict, Conan Doyle wrote in an undated letter:

… we have the expert's assertion that the figures were moving – I must confess that I have never seen any signs of this – and also the extreme naturalness of the figures.

It is hard to agree that the figures look 'natural,' but even as late as 1982, *The British Journal of Photography* stated:

… that with the camera they were using it would have been impossible to produce such clearly defined negatives …

It seems they too were ignorant of Snelling's intervention.

Back in 1920, Sir Arthur Conan Doyle wasn't really playing on a level field; the odds were already stacked against him, preventing him from coming to a rational explanation. In his haste to prove the existence of fairies, he may well have looked to Holmes' oft quoted dictum:

How often have I said to you that when you have eliminated the impossible, whatever remains, however improbable, must be the truth?

7 ELSIE AND FRANCES

One of Conan Doyle's deepest flaws was that he couldn't believe that Elsie and Frances – who he described as *children of the artisan class* – would have the brazen cheek to attempt to hoodwink a man of his superior class.

In 1917, when the girls first photographed the fairies, Elsie was fourteen and a half, and Frances was ten, (almost eleven) – although there is some confusion regarding this. Wikipedia gives Elsie's age as sixteen and in another article, her birth date as 1901, and other accounts give Elsie's age as seventeen. To be fair, there was another Elsie Wright born in Bradford in 1901, but she was not Arthur Wright's daughter.

The confusion over the girls' ages is even evident from Gardner. In his handwritten note dated July 25th. 1920, reprinted in an earlier chapter where he asks a series of questions on one side of the paper with the answers on the other, he gives their ages as seventeen and ten in answer to his question regarding when the photographs were taken. Gardner's original note appears to have been taken directly in answer to the questions he asked Arthur Wright in 1920. In much later typewritten note outlining the story, which was possibly written to gather his memories in preparation for his book published in 1945, Gardner records their ages in 1917 as being thirteen and ten, but there were four years between the cousins. The Cottingley photographs suggest the girls are older.

He wrote:

Story of the Fairy Photographs of 1920

May 1920

Print received fortnight later. Neg Mr Mann. Mr Snelling. Interview. Ilford enlargement for 'shading' Mortimer Hall EB and ACD (this was E. Blomfeld and her cousin Arthur Conan Doyle)

Interview ACD His article on F (fairies) *Agreement subject to Kodaks.*

Personal evidence essential. Visit to Cottingley and glen with

Elsie Wright 16, Frances Griffiths 13, (in 1917 13 and 10 when photos taken) Interview Mr Wright, Mrs W and Elsie. Conditions: No names, Yorkshire only. Neither fame nor money. Willing agai (here the typing goes off the small page).

ACD to Australia. E & F end of August Ensign cameras, (other accounts state he gave both girls folding Kodak Cameo cameras).

Marked plates.

Strand Xmas number.

Interviews.

Manchester Theatre.

Wakefield Town Hall.

Westminster Gazette.

Mr A P Sinner

Scotland and Ireland experiences.

In touch with the girls for ten years.

The coming of the Fairies ACD

Psychic test (Snelling)

America

Thought influences

Nature Spirits bodies'

Birth & death etc. ELG

With regard to Frances' age, by various accounts, the range runs from eight to eleven. Yet Elsie was born in 1903 and Frances in 1907 making Frances ten, (almost eleven), and Elsie fourteen and a half in mid 1917.

In looking at these girls with 21st century eyes, perhaps we deceive ourselves. Ten seems very young to us now, but this was a time when children routinely began working aged twelve.

Despite Conan Doyle's description of the girls as *children*, and referring to Elsie thus in a letter to her father:

I have seen the very interesting photo which your little girl

took ...

Elsie certainly wasn't a 'little girl,' and it is interesting to note that she had been attending Bradford Art College since the age of thirteen. Her ambition was to be a photographic colourist. At the time the Cottingley pictures were taken, she was already working for Gunstones Photographers, Manningham Lane, Bradford, spotting out white flaws on postcards for which she earned five shillings a week.

Both cousins were the only child within their respective

families. This was a highly unusual situation for that era when the majority of families of all classes boasted multiple offspring. Without siblings, the girls would have spent most of their time in adult company and it is likely they gained more sophistication from constant exposure to adult conversations and issues.

As Frances later said in an interview regarding her impression of Gardner:

[He] *had nothing much to say … and it made it very difficult for a little girl to talk … I had been brought up to make conversation with people – to keep the conversation going …*

Finally, both girls were comparatively well travelled. Elsie had spent time in Canada and Frances had been almost entirely raised in South Africa where she had lived a life of comparative luxury surrounded by servants. By the time their pictures became famous, the girls had already seen more of the world than any other average youngster in Cottingley.

Doyle wasn't emotionally fragile, but he was susceptible. The girls weren't scheming minxes, but they played their part.

The Cottingley locals treated the affair as a joke that had got out of hand.

But was there more to it?

8 THE MONEY

It is uncertain whether Gardner paid for the use of the photographs for his lecture tours, but considering what he was charging for reproductions: one shilling and sixpence for a small print and two shillings and sixpence for a large print, it is extremely likely some money made its way back to the Wright's household. Then, just as it got as good as seemed possible, they landed Sir Arthur Conan Doyle, the big fish they didn't expect to hook.

In June 1920, Doyle wrote the following to Gardner regarding the proposed trip to Cottingley:

If you go the Strand magazine would, of course, pay your expenses and say £25 more for the interview … why should you not get paid for such work?

Within that letter was a personal note to Arthur Wright:

Dear Mr Wright,

I have seen the very interesting photos which your little girl took.

They are certainly amazing. I was writing a little article for the Strand upon the evidence for the existence of fairies, so that I was very much interested. I should naturally like to use the photos, along with other material, in my article, but would not of course do so without your knowledge and permission. It would be in theChristmas number. I suggest:

1. That no name be mentioned, so that neither you nor your daughter be annoyed in any way.

2. That the use be reserved for the Strand only until Christmas. After that it reverts to you.

3. That either £5 be paid to you by the Strand for temporary use,

or that if you don't care to take money, you could be put on the free list of the magazine for three years. When the article appears in America in connection with Strand publications. I would, if you agree, try to get another £5 from that side. If this is agreeable to you I or my friend Mr Gardner would try to run up and have half an hour's chat with the girls.

Yours sincerely,

A. Conan Doyle

The five pounds was for the *temporary* use of the photographs and a further five pounds for temporary use in the American edition. That's somewhere in the region of two hundred and twenty five pounds sterling today and would have paid many months rent on a cottage back then.

If you recall, Wright originally refused payment. However, it soon becomes clear that money did indeed change hands. If you recall the letter in Gardner's papers, Arthur Wright names Garner as his sole agent and says:

Remuneration for this authority we agree to leave in his hands

He appears to be not overtly chasing the money, but he could have been fairly sure that an honourable man like Gardner would have looked after him financially.

Another letter in the same month of June 1920 from Doyle to Gardner runs thus:

… Then of the profits 50% should be mine and the remainder to be divided between you and the girls. That seems to me a fair division and I hope you will endorse it. We should look ahead

at this period for if the cinema proposition should have success we have a thing as marketable as the book. I think the parents should be told that we are setting apart a portion of the book for the girls and told that in dealing with the cinema we should also expect to have the handling of it and the right to use … might say 1/3 each of the profits.

It is well to be clear on it now as you never know what intrigues will arise and exaggerated statements and offers made.

In another letter, Doyle remarks to Gardner:

… But you <u>must</u> take another 10 guineas, whether you use it yourself or pass it on. I can't take money if you don't … Also I must deal fairly with Elsie and Mrs W.

In August 1920, again to Gardner, Doyle writes:

…I propose … if my magazine plans come off to set aside £100 for a wedding present and £50 for yourself to you as seems best to you.

And from Australia, Doyle wrote in October 1920:

Elsie's £100 should come equally or pro rata out of the … (words missing due to a hole in the paper) *… and other extras … We will suppose that my article cleared altogether £1,000 (a large supposition!) and yours £100 (it should be more much more). Ten if £200 comes out as I think we planned it would* *be £180 and £20, is that clear?*

What Doyle is saying is that he will donate £180 compared to Gardner's *pro rata* £20 to give £100 to Elsie. Whether the other £100 was for Polly Wright or Frances Griffiths, is unclear.

Gardner continued making small sums from the photographs and slides and presumably passing a portion of the money back to the families. In February 1921, he received two dollars with a request for the lantern slides from Chaplain H.H. Lippincott of the *USS Texas, 'cruising south of the equator.'*

In a letter to Gardner dated August 3rd 1921, Doyle writes:

I hope to get a small dowry for Elsie from the fairies. Also for the little girl.

That small dowry, the one hundred pounds would have been a small fortune and is now worth four and a half thousand pounds by 2017 standards. If you recall, at fourteen and a half, Elsie had been earning a mere five shillings a week.

With sums like this at stake, the pressure on the girls must have been enormous. However, they were not children. By 1920, Elsie was twenty and 'little' Frances thirteen – a full year older than many children in full time employment, and she would have been considered a young adult by the standards of her day.

It has been claimed that Arthur Wright refused to allow Elsie to benefit financially from the photographs, but that he held a War Bond for her for the £100. Doyle makes no mention of a war bond but Elsie still benefitted from Gardner's gifts such as the chocolates, (a real luxury in 1920), and of the camera, as her mother said:

Elsie is a very lucky girl!

9 CONFESSIONS

Sir Arthur Conan Doyle died in July 1930, aged 71, just one decade after the final three photographs of the Cottingley fairies had been taken. He left this world still believing in fairies and confident of the afterlife. So many mourners attended his funeral – over eight thousand – it was held at The Royal Albert Hall in London.

After Doyle's death, interest in the Cottingley affair appears to have died down. This could be in part because Gardner barred access to his papers. He had made the matter famous in the first place and possibly recalling how he had been cast aside by Hodson at Cottingley, was in no mood to share it.

However there may have been a darker side to his motives: he was the one person who had ordered the plates to be 'enhanced' to make the fairies look more 3D and as real as possible and as technology improved it made the prospect of discovery and it was he who would have been accused of fraud.

In 1945, when he was well into his seventies, Gardner published his own account of the Cottingley Fairies entitled *Fairies: A Book of Real Fairies,* but it added very little to Doyle's account that appeared in his own book *The Coming of the Fairies.*

Just as Gardner was preparing his final book, *Pictures of Fairies: The Cottingley Photographs* in 1965, a newspaper found Elsie living in Nottingham. She was in her sixties by then and must have thought she was safe from any further interest.

Elsie had worked in many jobs all using her artistic skills and had eventually left Cottingley for America to escape all the fuss. There she met her husband Frank Hill, a Scottish engineer on leave from India. They married and lived in India until 1949. Her mother, Polly had written to Gardner telling him how happy Elsie was with her new life in India and that she was expecting a baby.

After the Declaration of Independence and the handing over of power b the British to India in 1947, the couple returned to England and settled in Nottingham with their only child, a son called Glenn. Polly died in 1956 at the age of 79 after being looked after by Elsie. When asked about the fairy photographs, Elsie stated she wanted the matter to be buried and said that people should make up their own minds.

For her part, Frances returned to live in South Africa where she married in 1928. Her husband was a Warrant Officer and they had two children, Christine and David. When Frances' husband, Sydney retired from the army, the family returned to England and lived in Ramsgate on the south coast. There seems to have been little or no contact between France and Elsie.

Gardner's last book, *Pictures of Fairies, the Cottingley Photographs* was published by the Theosophical Publishing House in 1966. Back then the photographs had still not been found to be fakes and his book was a success and once again, the world was entranced by the story of the girls and the fairies at the beck.

Three years later, in 1969, Edward Lewis Gardner died, aged 100, at the Theosophical Home for the elderly. He left all the material in the care of his son Leslie with strict instructions to keep the negatives and photographs safely away from any scrutiny.

The death of Gardner once again attracted interest in the case but it took another two years before BBC's programme *Nationwide* interviewed Elsie in her home and Frances who was by then a matron at Epsom College.

Elsie had not wanted to upset Doyle or Gardner, but even though they were now both dead, she made no confession. She simply said:

… let's say they are figments of our imagination, Frances and mine and leave it at that.

Frances added nothing of interest and so the mystery continued.

In 1973 Stewart Sanderson of the English Department at Leeds University and President of the Folklore Society, persuaded Gardner's son Leslie, then in his 80's, to donate his father's correspondence to the Brotherton Collection at Leeds University. Badly stored in an old blue, suitcase, by now some of the letters were damp and had partly disintegrated.

Leslie Gardner also donated five glass plates which he understood to be the originals of the photos. On examination, it was found that the original prints had not been developed from these negatives.

In 1976, Yorkshire Television decided to take the now elderly ladies – Elsie was 75 and Frances 69 – back to the beck. It was to be the first time they had been together in Cottingley since the 1920's, but even after all this time, they remained evasive. There was a strong undercurrent of distrust between them. Perhaps they both finally understood the story was never going to simply go away and could well have decided to exploit separate money-making opportunities through the renewed interest in their fairy story. Frances certainly discussed the possibility with author Joe Cooper.

After the programme, they never appeared on TV together again.

Fred Gettings, was an expert on occult art who wrote many books. His *Ghosts in Photographs: The Extraordinary Story of Spirit Photography,* was published in 1978 and covers the Cottingley case. It was whilst gathering material for this book in 1977, that he stumbled upon the source of the fairies. The template for the fairy images was a line of dancing girls from the 1914 edition of *The Princess Mary Gift Book,* a popular publication, produced to raise money for the war effort.

When compared side by side it is evident the *Princess Mary Gift Book* figures are not identical to the Cottingley fairies, but they are very close copies:

Elsie's son Glenn confronted her with Gettings' findings and Elsie confessed Frances had brought her copy of *The Princess Mary Gift Book* with her when she came to Cottingley from South Africa in 1917. It was she, Elsie, the family artist, who had traced the picture and added wings to the figures.

In a later interview she appeared very proud of her handiwork:

… they were luminous the Kodak man said and they were
moving and because I was quite good at drawing and painting
at school and I'd been to the art school, the teacher said I must
have drawn and painted them myself and cut them out and put
them in the grass, but they enlarged them. Oh, to the size of
half a house nearly, looking for brush marks and paint marks to
see if they could see any trace of art work on them and they
couldn't find that.

Elsie must have contacted Frances and told her because Frances
heard she had confessed to her son. This freed up Frances to
share the truth too. She admitted almost everything to Joe
Cooper who was writing a book about Cottingley and who
hitherto had passionately believed the photographs to be true.
However, perhaps because she did not want to let him down
entirely, Frances still insisted that the fifth photograph was real.
She said:

It was a wet Saturday afternoon and we were just mooching
about with our cameras and Elsie had nothing prepared. I saw
these fairies building up in the grasses and just aimed the
camera and took a photograph.

Even with this scrap of hope, the effect on Joe was devastating.

Joe Cooper had been a lecturer in sociology at Bradford University. He was interested in astrology and the occult and wrote books on the paranormal. The previous year, in 1976, he had met a lady from Cottingley who remarked that she knew the ladies who had taken the photographs. Joe was intrigued and the lady put him in contact with Elsie and Frances.

Joe an engaging eccentric, had been interested in the Cottingley story for years. With access to the original participants his interest quickly became an obsession. He racked up thousands of miles shuttling between Elsie and Frances, one in Nottingham, the other in Ramsgate who by then they were barely talking to each other.

When Frances initially made her semi-admission, poor Joe had a crisis and became ill. According to his ex-wife Shirley, he had something of a nervous breakdown and the hoax cost him his marriage. He went missing for nine months. Shirley contacted Frances who said bluntly:

I haven't seen him since I told him they were fakes ...

For more than fifty years Elsie and Frances had kept their secret. They had not wanted to reveal the truth until all of the principals in the case had passed away. Of these, it was Sir Arthur Conan Doyle who they had been most concerned about. They did not want to embarrass him when it came out that the photographs were not real. Or perhaps they were simply nervous as to his reaction and the legal and financial implications. Of the original players in the story, only Hodson was still alive but both Elsie and Frances owed him nothing and considered him to be a fake. So they were not too worried about hurting either his feelings or his reputation.

Hodson had been wrong about the photographs and in his assessment of the honesty of the girls. Now old ladies, Elsie and Frances admitted that they had teased Hodson terribly and had a lot of fun at his expense during his entire stay. They were highly amused by his gullible attitude and had spent their time pointing out non-existent fairies – which he then claimed to have seen as well. This had only egged them on to make even more outrageous 'sightings.' To their astonishment, their wildest pranks were calmly received by the clairvoyant who agreed he could also see whatever the girls told him they saw, and more.

Perhaps Hodson's ego had got the better of him? It is possible that his reputation as a well-respected expert in the field meant he could not allow himself to be outdone by a couple of girls. In his opinion, nature spirits were not visible on the physical plane and he believed his powers to be considerably greater than the girls, so it is possible that he had imaginary experiences that seemed genuine to him.

After his Cottingley experience he went on to write many books on clairvoyance. In early 1983, when he was 96 and living in New Zealand, Hodson finally heard the about the confessions and became the only surviving member of Doyle's and Gardner's team to know the truth.

By then, it was possibly too upsetting for Hodson to admit he had been wrong all those years before and accept the scale of the fraud and how cruel those seemingly sweet girls had been to him. Less than a month after discovering the truth, Geoffrey Hodson died on 23rd January 1983 at the age of 96.

At age 75, Frances was the first to make a wholly public confession which appeared after Hodson's death in *The Times* on the 9th. of April 1983. She said:

I'm fed up with all these stories... I hated those photographs and cringe every time I see them. I thought it was a joke, but everyone else kept it going. It should have died a natural death 60 years ago.

Frances recalled how paper cut-outs and hatpins had been used, but she still insisted that the last photograph, *The Fairy Sunbath* was of real fairies, taken by her.

Elsie aged 81, found herself suddenly besieged by reporters at her Nottingham home. She maintained that all five photographs were of cut-outs, and that she had drawn all the fairies figures on stiff paper including the ones in the last photo, the one Frances claimed was real.

She explained how she had cut them out using sharp tailor's scissors, borrowed from Frances's mother, who worked as a tailor in Bradford. The images were secured in place by long hatpins and fastened with zinc oxide bandage tape to a bank of earth or bushes. Then a gentle breeze had set their paper wings a-fluttering – hence the 'movement' Harold Snelling, the photographic expert, had detected.

Regarding *The Fairy Sunbath*, she was sure *she* had taken it. Frances had not even been there at the time it had been taken so she was sure it was her shot. However, it seems there was some confusion about which plates had been used and the final photograph is a simple double exposure.

In theory, both of them could have taken it.

Slowly, Joe Cooper recovered. Although he exposed Frances and Elsie's deception in a magazine called *The Unexplained* in 1983, he still embraced an unshakeable belief in fairies. He painstakingly built up a considerable body of research for his 1990 book, *The Case of the Cottingley Fairies*.

Eventually Joe was considered such an expert on the affair that he became an advisor on the 1997 film *Fairy Tale: A True Story*. Reading Joe's book, it is easy to see that he was squarely with Conan Doyle and also strongly felt the need for there to be more of *a glamour and mystery to life.* His book starts with such high hopes and ends wryly. Despite all the accusations of fakery over the years, the cousins had insisted the photographs were real and right up until the last moment, Joe had sincerely believed them. Despite what must have been a crushing disappointment, Joe gallantly dedicated his book to Elsie and Frances and described them as being:

… two amiable adventuresses.

However, his ex-wife claimed Joe's encounter with Elsie and Frances left him a changed man. She said:

They watched him devote years of his life to all that research, going back and forth to them both. I think it was a power thing with them. I met Elsie once and she couldn't look me in the eye … Sixty five years after those photographs were taken, they ended my marriage. When I heard plans about a statue of Elsie and Frances, I thought; 'Please, no.' I don't want them glorified.

Photographic expert Geoffrey Crawley was the first person to bring modern techniques to bear upon the Cottingley photographs. He acquired the original cameras and began testing them to see if they could produce the kind of sharply defined negatives Doyle had been presented with. They could not and it soon became clear that Snelling's enhancements had been quite dramatic. They had transmuted pale blurs into the celebrated fairies. Even so, Crawley retained his admiration for

73

what the girls had achieved. He wrote this in the *British
Journal of Photography*:

Elsie gave us a myth which has never harmed anyone.

Adding:

*How many professed photographers, can claim to have
equalled her achievement with the first photograph they
ever took?*

In that much disputed fifth picture, *The Fairies Sunbath*, under
close scrutiny two human faces appear in the grass to the right
of the fairy figures. Both Elsie and Frances claimed they took it
and as mentioned previously, perhaps they both did. It was
Geoffrey Crawley who discovered it was a double exposure.

As late as 2010, the photographs were still causing controversy.
Following Crawley's obituary in *The Times*, Stewart Sanderson,
(the man who had persuaded Gardner's son to donate his
father's letters to the Brotherton Library at Leeds University),
wrote claiming Geoffrey Crawley's 1983 article had been based
upon his 1973 talk where he revealed Elsie's artistic talents.

After all the deceptions and half-told truths, the consensus is
that the girls faked the pictures for their own reasons. Elsie was
trying to keep Frances from being beaten for continually falling
in the beck and Frances wanted to show her mother that fairies

really existed and she had been wrong to laugh at her.

It would have remained within the family but for Polly's interest in Theosophy. The story was then taken up by firm believers – the 'real perpetrators' in many peoples' opinion – and the almost-innocent young girls were swept along by the sheer force of public interest. Worse yet, as their fairy story gained an unimagined momentum, the involvement of Sir Arthur Conan Doyle and all the subsequent publicity made it impossible for them to back track and admit it was all a hoax gone wrong.

Doyle's fame and sincere belief in Spirituality blinded him to the possibility that the photographs could be fakes and he dismissed the idea that people of a lower class would ever want to deceive him. His love for his father and his family's interest in fairy art and lore spurred a deep need within him to secure proof of fairy existence. His books and articles spread the word – and the fraud – throughout the world.

The only person suspicious from the outset was Elsie's father, Arthur Wright. He seemed to know the girls had faked the photographs somehow and he could not understand why someone as seemingly intelligent as Doyle would believe they were truly fairies. He considered Elsie had not been very bright at school and it amazed him that she had fooled the creator of the world's greatest detective.

Gardner and Barlow were caught up in their own enthusiasm and even Snelling, the man who fatally doctored the originals to make them look more life-like was a firm believer. Polly and Annie were just loving mothers who wanted to think the best of their children, fully believing their daughters were telling the truth and they really had photographed fairies at the beck.

This is the accepted version. But it is wrong.

10 THE REVEAL

Once it is accepted that the photographs are a fraud, further inconsistencies become evident.

If you recall there is the problematic statement early on from Edie Wright that both girls had played with the fairies at the beck *since babyhood.* The anomaly is recorded in Gardner's note from 1920:

How long seen fairies? Many years

This was not possible; it might be a stretch to argue that Elsie could not have done this as she had only been away in Canada for four years – she still had other years in which to interact with the fairies at the beck.

Yet Frances could not have seen them *since babyhood* as she had only just come to live in Cottingley after being raised in South Africa. It was sloppy of both Gardner and Doyle not to have noticed this.

There are other discrepancies. If you recall Arthur Wright's original statement:

... It was about 1 o'clock that I put just one plate in the box and gave it to Elsie ...

and

... my wife says the children were not gone an hour before they brought the camera in saying they had taken a photograph.

Therefore the first picture would have been taken at around 2.00pm, but according to Gardner's notes, it wasn't taken until 3.30pm, a full hour and a half later:

Dates of 2 photos	*July 1917*	*Sept 1917*
Times of day	*3.30*	*5.00*

Conan Doyle insisted on using aliases for the girls, (Elsie became Iris and Frances, Alice), concerned that *a hundred charabancs* would descend upon the Beck. But his subterfuge was in vain, somehow the story leaked and within *a week* reporters from national newspapers had found their way to Cottingley. If more interest ultimately resulted in more revenue, it is not difficult to imagine the source of that leak.

It is ironic that with hindsight, the 'evidence' of Kenneth Styles the psychic, sent to Conan Doyle in 1920 might not be entirely wrong. If you recall, he said:

... Re photographs; the more I think of it the less I like it. My own controls say it was taken by a fair man with his hair brushed back. He has a studio with a lot of cameras some of which are turned by a handle. He did it to please the little girl in the picture who writes fairy stories which he illustrates in this fashion.

This could be Harold Snelling, the photographic re-toucher. He would have had a studio and presumably more than one camera, yet photographs of him are very hard to find and I cannot determine if he was fair or not.

Arthur Wright's photographs show him as a dark man with his hair brushed back; although this photographer's own photographs aren't clear and his hair may have been oiled dark. He hadn't a studio as suggested, but he did have a dark room. As for owning 'a lot' of cameras, Polly's letter to Gardner certainly suggests he owned more than one:

… The camera you so kindly sent is fine, far better than those we have.

The little girl was Frances, not his daughter, and the only fairy tales she told were about the validity of the photographs which perhaps he did indeed illustrate!

However …

The newly rediscovered evidence is so strong it relegates all the previous points to mere supporting players in the argument.

There is an image of another girl gazing on as fairies dance around her. It was taken in 1918, a little after the Cottingley photographs. Its execution is poor and lacking Snelling's skills, the pale fairies seem out of place against the dark background. It looks like a direct copy of *Frances and the Dancing Fairies*, the first Cottingley photograph, the one with Frances. It has appeared online where it has been described as 'a bad copy.'

I have been able to find very little about its creator, Dorothy Inman, who died without revealing how she made it. It is held in the same collection as the Cottingley fairy material where it is labelled *Mrs Inman's Fake Photograph*. It appeared in an exhibition about fairies held in Brighton Museum in 1980, but frustratingly, there is very little other information to be had about it.

Sometime in the summer of 1917 another fairy photograph was taken of another child. This picture was taken in a London garden and it was printed in 1918 in a popular magazine called *The Sphere*, a heavily illustrated publication akin to the *Illustrated London News*.

This photograph was published under the heading, *A Fantastic Invasion of a Modern Garden*, with this printed beneath it:

An attempt to picture the Little Folk, with which a child will people even the most prosaic London garden, and the little girl who loved them.

The girl is seated before paper cut outs of fairies adorning a hedge. It would seem that the Cottingley photographs spawned a couple of keen imitators.

Or did they?

We have only the Wright and Griffiths' families' word that the girls took the Cottingley photographs in 1917. The photographs were not seen by the wider world until 1919 and certainly not published until late 1920. Going by provable evidence, and not just the claims of the Wright and Griffiths families, both Dorothy Inman's and *The Sphere's* photographs *pre-date* the Cottingley fairy photographs.

What if the Cottingley photographs were *copies of these images?*

The pictures of Dorothy, the girl in the London garden and Frances are similar enough to stretch the boundaries of coincidence. By everyone insisting the first two Cottingley pictures were taken in 1917, it could only mean one thing…

The adults were an integral part of the conspiracy and Arthur Wright, far from being the sceptic, was embedded at the heart of the deception.

It would mean that his claims that he and Polly had searched the girls' attic bedroom and the beck for evidence of fakery but found none, were also untrue.

It is likely that Arthur Wright came across *The Sphere's* photograph, (it was a popular magazine of its time), or Dorothy Inman's picture or even *both* and decided he could do better. It is also possible that in showing the Cottingley photographs to the Theosophists, his wife Polly deliberately set out to bring their pictures to as wide an audience as possible.

Although Box Brownie cameras were manufactured cheaply and actively marketed at that time as being for the use of children, Midg cameras were trickier to use. Could it be that Arthur Wright, the keen amateur photographer, did more than merely develop the glass plates? In their summation of the photographs, Kodak stated that an *experienced photographer* may have been involved.

Could Arthur have taken the pictures? It's an intriguing thought that has often been raised. With this new possibility that Arthur may have been lying about the date of the first two photographs, it makes it likelier that he was also concealing the truth about their true author.

The very earliest reference to the Cottingley photographs being shared outside the immediate family was when Frances Griffiths sent a letter to a friend in South Africa, dated November 9, 1918, still long after Inman's and *The Sphere* photographs, Frances included a photograph of the fairies, and wrote:

I am sending two photos, both of me, one of me in a bathing costume in our back yard, Uncle Arthur took that, while the other is me with some fairies up the beck, Elsie took that one.

On the back of photograph, Frances has written:

Elsie and I are very friendly with the beck Fairies. It is funny I never used to see them in Africa. It must be too hot for them there.

The date of the letter is still some months after *The Sphere* picture was published, and Frances seems determined to stress that *Elsie* took the fairy picture, not Arthur, perhaps her unnecessary assertion seems a little artificial.

There is no argument that the third, fourth and intriguing fifth photographs, known as *The Fairies Sunbath* had been taken as late as 1920, long after the Inman and *The Sphere* images appeared, but this raises a further question: if the girls were pretending the fairies were so prevalent around the Beck why wait *three years* to get more pictures of them?

Also, why – and this is surely a critical observation – has no-one ever noticed that the girls don't seem to have grown any older in the second set of pictures?

Arthur was always the sceptic and Polly the enthusiast. Could it have all been part of an act to convince people? Were they deliberately playing opposing roles in a metaphysical version of *Good Cop/Bad Cop?*

Unlike poor Hodson, it would appear Doyle had not been hoodwinked by two mischievous girls, but was the victim of a group of cunning adults.

In the two letters Polly wrote to Gardner within a few days of one another in July 1920 concerning the camera he had sent, Polly employs the following expression:

I do hope Elsie will be able to take <u>some photos of the kind you want</u>.

And in the second letter:

I hope it isn't long before we can send you <u>some photos of the kind you want</u>...

In neither case does she specifically mention fairy photographs. You might be familiar with the term *embedded confessions* in the relatively new science of Statement Analysis; in SA, such deliberate avoidance of an obvious and more exact term – in this case, *fairy photographs,* is regarded as highly suspicious. It is noticeable that Polly avoids specific, written mention of fairy photographs twice within a few days. Such evasion is suggestive of Polly's direct and knowing involvement in the deception.

It could be Polly's personal way of expressing herself, but she cannot have been averse to mentioning fairies as it was she who initially brought the photographs to the attention of the Theosophical Society.

What of Polly's part in bringing the pictures to the attention of the Theosophists? It is possible that fairies were mentioned at that meeting, but what if she had instigated the discussion, and guided it so she could unveil photographs that were so amazing but that had been left gathering dust in a drawer?

This is a mere aside, but some reports claim she was carrying the two year old photographs in her handbag. Fairies or not, most mothers update pictures of their children regularly – at that time, just after the war, old photographs were objects of great sadness as they usually indicated the sitter had died. With a photographer for a husband, Polly would have had more opportunity than most to have new photographs taken of her daughter and niece.

Polly's friend, Edie Wright, had also played her part. Even though she had left the Theosophists for 'private reasons' by the time the Cottingley photographs were first seen, she was the one who aided Polly in answering Gardner's initial letter and it was she who sent him the plates. What if those 'private reasons' for leaving had left her bearing a grudge? If so, her part in the deception, and in particular making a fool of such a luminary as Edward Gardner, could well have represented some kind of personal pay back for her.

Please remember, all I am presenting here is conjecture. Although I believe my argument is compelling, I cannot *prove* who took the Cottingley photographs or when. No one can. I am just bringing your attention to other, similar images that provably predate the Cottingley ones in terms of publication.

I find it wonderful that even after a hundred years the Cottingley fairies are still deceiving us all. The only thing for sure is that a century on, the Cottingley photographs are still raising questions.

10 POSTSCRIPT: MODERN FAIRIES

There have been modern versions of The Cottingley Fairy photographs, the two most famous both involve people I am proud to call friends.

Prominent amongst recent hoaxes is the story concerning Dan Baines. In 2004, Dan, then working in forensics, decided to stage a prank. He bought a miniature plastic skeleton from a joke shop and wrapped it in soggy tissue which he painted brown. A few skeletonised leaves made suitably ragged looking wings and lo! he had created a mummified fairy.

Dan's wife, Monique donned latex gloves and she held the figurine in her cupped palms over an official looking police evidence bag. The photo was taken and the trap was set.

Dan published the sensational picture onto the net just as America was waking up. When people read the story of how a dog walker from the Derbyshire town of Bacup had discovered the tiny figure lying by an Iron age barrow, how *scientists are baffled* and *it's bones are hollow it would have been capable of flight,* they scrambled to share the story on social media.

Within hours, Dan's *Mummified Fairy* had gone viral. Unable to cope with the barrage of messages, over 24,000 in an unfeasibly short space of time, his email toppled. Many people warned him to take the fairy back to its resting place or he would face terrible consequences. The fairy appeared in newspapers and magazines and Dan was in demand for newspaper, television and radio interviews.

A month later, on the appropriate day, Dan announced, *'April Fool!'* and exposed his story as a hoax.

He was not prepared for what happened next.

He faced a storm of abuse as angry believers turned on him. He was accused of spreading disinformation and of working on behalf of the government – this, at least was true, at that time, Dan *did* work for the government.

After many verbal drubbings, Dan was dismayed to discover that the new forensics job he had landed was his no more. His employers held strong religious beliefs and considered he would no longer be seen as a credible witness when bringing forensic evidence into a witness box. They cited Dan's prank as showing *an unhealthy interest in the occult.*

Thankfully Dan Baines is a resourceful chap, and he saw an opportunity to turn the situation around. He began using his creative talents to design magic tricks such as the gruesome *Dolly Darko*. He now has a thriving business and his pieces have travelled world wide. Some have been snapped up by the film director Guillermo del Torro and are displayed in his famous *Bleak House* in Los Angeles. At time of writing Del Torro is touring parts of *Bleak House* as an exhibition – and the exhibit includes some of Dan's work. In organising *Doomsday*

North, and asking me to speak there, Dan was also the unwitting instigator of this book.

Because of my involvement with the Faery Festival, I have been sent some interesting pictures such as this one where leaf litter combined with light reflections appears to form a winged figure with arms outstretched. My Granny would insist it was a fairy, and some would say that nature spirits use whatever they can to manifest.

In 2014, the then Manchester based artist, John Hyatt was enjoying a walk in the Rossendale valley when he photographed a cloud of insects. Upon closer inspection, the insects appeared to be tiny, winged figures.

I was out with my camera deliberately trying to photograph fast moving things. I went back home and looked at the computer

92

and then I realised what I'd photographed.

John is unwilling to admit or deny his images are of fairies. He gave a talk at *The Oxford Natural History Museum* where the verdict was that the photographs are of insects. John says he has deliberately avoided revealing his own opinion because he is far more interested in other people's reaction to his photographs. He said:

I went out for the next few days and took more photographs but every photograph that I took looked like insects.

I first met John when he exhibited his extraordinary images at the *Whitaker Rossendale Museum and Art Gallery*. He told me that just like the *Mummified Fairy*, his pictures had also gone viral. Television stations in Japan had been contacting him and takings at the Whitaker had increased by 600% during his show.

Now based in *Liverpool John Moore's University*, at that time John was a professor of Art and Design at *Manchester Metropolitan University*. He too faced a barrage of queries from people all over the world asking him how to contact fairies. He said:

Some lads in Israel asked me for my advice on how to go and find fairies. I gave them my advice and some tips on how to use a camera and they sent me some in Israel.

John has been careful not to reveal the precise location of his picture saying:

I won't be more specific because I don't want people going and trashing it. You'd be surprised at how many people have told me they want to go there.

John began researching fairy lore and discovered that in many legends, the original fairies in Britain weren't tiny but human-sized and lived in the forests. Rossendale was originally all forest. He also discovered that traditionally fairies were seen as harbingers of misfortune.

… fairies symbolise death as they are creatures from the other side. Certainly, in a lot of fairytales they are dangerous … The day it went viral I was diagnosed with throat cancer so it was quite interesting in a sense that for the first month of the fairies going viral I didn't have any time to worry about having throat

cancer because I was talking to people all around the world.

The interesting thing is that the people who didn't believe were very abusive and felt that their world was threatened – if they didn't have a very rigid attitude to reality, everything would crumble.

I am delighted to report that John has since made a full recovery.

It is a strange coincidence that for us three, since we dabbled in the realm of fairy, everything has changed. Dan's now doing the work he loves, John has moved to Liverpool and is cancer free and I am pursuing a writing career.

The one thing we have in common is that we could all say the fairies have been exceptionally good to us.

Be it *The Cottingley Fairies, The Last Changeling, The Mummified Fairy* or *The Rossendale Fairies,* the public response to anything involving fairies is still extraordinary. It is heartening to reflect that even now in the twenty first century, people can still be children at heart and that fairies can still capture the mass imagination with their indefinable allure.

ABOUT THE AUTHOR

F.R. Maher is the author of the fantasy thriller novel about dark fairies *The Last Changeling* and the *Horror in a Hurry* series of novellas. She has written for the Twitter group #FolkloreThursday and regularly contributes to magazines such as *Waiting* and *The Fortean Times*. She also organises *The Legendary Llangollen Faery Festival* and the *Cogwarts Steampunk Spectacular* weekend.

www.northwalesfaeryfestival.com

www.thelastchangeling.com

26362115R00063

Printed in Poland
by Amazon Fulfillment
Poland Sp. z o.o., Wrocław